101 Days of Inspiration
Accelerate Your Spiritual Growth

HCP
BOOK PUBLISHING

God's Image Jamaica
PUBLICATION

C. Orville McLeish

ISBN-13: 978-1-958404-15-7 (paperback)

First Edition.

You can visit the Author Website @ https://corvillemcleish.com/

For those whose sole desire is to become a full manifestation of God's intent when He said, "Let Us make man in Our image and likeness…" visit our YouTube page @ God's Image Jamaica (God's Image Jamaica - YouTube). Let us change the world one maturing soul at a time!

Daily Reminder

...man shall not live by bread alone; but man lives by every word that proceeds from the mouth of the Lord. (Deuteronomy 8:3b).

Day 1
Run Your Race

Do not remember the former things, nor consider the things of old. Behold, I will do a new thing, now it shall spring forth; shall you not know it? I will even make a road in the wilderness and rivers in the desert. (Isaiah 43:18-19).

Run the race that is set before you with perseverance. Do not give up. Focus on the finish line and make strides towards it. You will not only get there, but you will finish this race. Adapt a spirit of finishing. Whatever you start, don't stop and detour from it until you see it to completion. You are a finisher. Leave nothing half done. Draw from the deep reservoir of possibilities that God has placed inside you.

You have the potential to rise above everything that would oppose you or seek to slow you down. Speak to your mountains. Command them to move out of your way. Lift your hands in worship over the Red Seas in your life and watch the waters part. You will run on dry ground; your feet will not get wet with the mire of this life. The path to success is laid out before you, so simply walk in it with favour, not fear. Do not settle. Go for the gold. You deserve it.

Day 2
Finishing Strong

Let your eyes look straight ahead, and your eyelids look right before you. (Proverbs 4:25).

There is a stallion in you, for though you may feel weak, keep affirming that you are strong. The strength of the Lord will be made perfect in your weakness. He will supplement what is lacking, if you put your trust in Him. Those whose hearts are stayed on Jesus will find immeasurable peace, under any circumstances.

You will not be overcome by the waves of the sea or the storms that threaten to shatter your dreams. Storms will come, but only to make you stronger. You will not die in your suffering but will walk away a victor. That is what you possess. The kingdom of God is in you. The ability to finish strong is already embedded in your DNA. Simply believe and do not allow yourself to be overcome with doubt. Doubt will derail you, but faith will keep you in line and you will overcome because that is who you are.

Day 3
Follow the Leader

Jesus said to him, "I am the way, the truth, and the life. No one comes to the Father except through Me." (John 14:6).

The greatest leaders are usually excellent followers, but the transition requires a process. We must subscribe to the process, embrace it and allow God to walk us through it. Don't ask God to do a quick work in you, but allow Him to process you in His own timing. He knows exactly what you need. He knows what needs to be removed from your life and what will be permitted to stay.

It is in difficult times that we are purged, purified and made into gold. There is no other means of purification except by fire…but as you walk through the fire, God will be there. When you walk through the flood, God will be there. It doesn't matter what you are going through, God is with you. Follow Him. Don't walk after others who are also being processed. Can the blind lead the blind? Follow after God. Become a man/woman after God's own heart.

Day 4
The Black Dot

They are abundantly satisfied with the fullness of Your house, and You give them drink from the river of Your pleasures. (Psalms 36:8).

There is a story of a professor who handed a test paper to his students and asked them to write on it what they could see. At the centre of the test paper was a dot. Students wrote differently describing the dot. At the end of the test, the professor read what they had written aloud. He asked why no one described the white space but all focused on the small back dot. "That's more like our life," he said. "We focus on the little black dot forgetting the abundance life has offered and has to offer. We magnify the little black dots in our lives that we forget the white space. We forget that there is more to the test paper than the black dot. It is only when you see beyond the dot that you can appreciate the test paper."

Open your mind and visualize the abundant opportunities in the "white spaces" of life. It is a paper first before the dot. The dot does not define it, at least not totally, until you magnify it. Accept that the dot is part of the test but not the whole picture. By focusing on and magnifying your challenges, you lose sight and hold of life itself. You see less and less of the vast opportunities and choices that are abundantly available. Today, enjoy, explore, and embrace the rest of the space. Stop magnifying the little black dots in your life and start enjoying the white spaces you have.

Day 5
Say Yes to Your Dream

Ask, and it will be given to you; seek, and you will find; knock, and it will be opened to you. (Matthew 7:7).

Approve of your dream, pursue a worthy goal, and have a larger vision of yourself. Stop wallowing, get out of self-pity and start saying yes to your amazing dream. Many walk through life feeling lifeless and uncommitted to their dream. They have great desires to make certain changes to their present situations but refuse to welcome their dreams of making things work for them. Some have great jobs but know deep inside them that that is not where they should be. Many desire a great home but are not committed to making things work.

Dreams are only dreams if you don't work on them to become a reality. Do you have certain dreams that have been shelved for reasons you cannot explain? Your dream may be to lose some weight around your belly, to travel the world, to change jobs and pursue a carrier, or to build a home. If you must experience the true greatness you are made for, start saying yes to your dreams and embrace a life of possibilities.

Day 6
Best Medicine for Painful Circumstances

But I want you to know, brethren, that the things which happened to me have actually turned out for the furtherance of the gospel. And most of the brethren in the Lord, having become confident by my chains, are much more bold to speak the word without fear. (Philippians 1:14).

Never let the light of your countenance be dimmed by your circumstance. Smile as much as you can. Laugh every chance you get. Cry when you have to, but do not dwell in your pain. The circumstance may be painful; however, the pain is not you, and neither does it represent who you are. Pain cannot define who you are. It is a vehicle to get you somewhere, but it is never your destination. If you stop feeding it with the food of your thoughts, it will pass away.

Laughter is good medicine. This is literal, not metaphorical. Laughter signifies that your perception of difficulty is divine, not earthly. Pain desires for you to respond a certain way. It wants you to be sour, depressed, and despondent. Why not give it a different response?

Day 7
Love Those Around You

A new commandment I give to you, that you love one another; as I have loved you, that you also love one another. By this all will know that you are My disciples, if you have love for one another. (John 13:34-35).

It is not by miracles that people know we belong to God. It is not determined by how many years we have been a member of a church or the positions we hold or have held. Our affiliation with God is measured by our capacity to love those in our area of influence. Love is our true power, and by extending love, we extend God to others.

People do crazy things in the name of love. Often what they perceive as love is not even the real thing because it is skewed by selfishness and desires not in line with divine realities. God is love. Those who love, know God. Those who know not love does not know God. Love even has a greater power because it is the only thing, when perfected, that can drive out fear. Do you want to live free from fear? Love perfected in you is the key. True love is the God-kind of love, and you have the capacity to share that with the world.

Day 8
Bounce Back

For a righteous man may fall seven times and rise again, but the wicked shall fall by calamity. (Proverbs 24:16).

There is a saying "Saints are just sinners who fall down and get back up." Falling is not as important as what you do afterward. Are you plagued by habitual sin? Do you experience condemnation and guilt as soon as you partake in the act? Have you tried everything to be free but just cannot find the measure of freedom you believe a child of God should have? Welcome to the club! Don't be fooled by those who pretend like they never fall. If you keep getting back up, you will get God's attention. God will honour the one who never gives up.

No one is perfect. Our perfection is a garment that God provides for us to wear. It was His idea, not ours. He loved you before you even knew He had His eyes on you. He is not moved by your weakness and failure to live righteous in your own strength and effort. He knows our greatest attempt at righteousness is like filthy rags. Yet, every time you get back up, as long as you don't withhold forgiveness from others who also fall, God will receive you and accept you as if you did not fall. This is what it means to be justified. God will restore you a million times if He has to so you can continue your journey. Rest in His love and keep your eyes on Him. Eventually, everything that is not a reflection of who He is will begin to slither away and disappear. Your comeback will be greater than your setback.

Day 9
Stand Out of the Crowd

For as he thinks in his heart, so is he. "Eat and drink!" he says to you, but his heart is not with you. (Proverbs 23:7).

You were not created to fit in but to stand out. You are as unique in this world as your DNA and fingerprint. What you carry and have to offer is exclusive only to you. No one can replace you or take your place. Give knowing you have something of great value to offer. Your time, talents, abilities, and resources are extra-ordinary. Don't compare yourself to others. Everyone's journey is not the same.

Learn to live from the inside out. God lives inside you, and He knows you better than you know yourself. He has the blueprint for your life. He knows where you are going and what the expected end will look like for you. You are not just being or doing, but you are becoming. There is a greater version of you in the future that far exceeds any request you can make or image you can conjure up in your mind. Don't allow outside influences to dictate the posture of your heart and the quality of your thoughts. Greater is He who is inside you than anything on the outside. Be secure in being different.

Day 10
Let Nothing Separate You From God

For I am persuaded that neither death nor life, nor angels nor principalities nor powers, nor things present nor things to come, nor height nor depth, nor any other created thing, shall be able to separate us from the love of God which is in Christ Jesus our Lord. (Romans 8:38-39).

In God you live, move, breathe, and have your being. There is nothing in and outside this world that can separate you from God. He is as close to you as the air you breathe. God is the air you breathe. You are held together by His Word and the breath from His mouth. As the Spirit hovered over the waters in Genesis, so does He hover over you. So when God speaks a word over you, it will manifest. No matter what you are going through, it is well, and it shall be well.

Love does not exist outside of God because God is love. The world was built on the foundation of love. God became a man because of love. He never turned His back on His creation when they fell in Genesis, and He surely will not turn His back on you. He can't. They say nothing is impossible for God, but is this really true? It seems impossible for God to act contrary to His Word. It is also impossible for God to lie. If He says He will bring you through, then the outcome of your battles is already decided no matter the intensity of all that is working against you. Rest in His promises. You are going to be okay.

Day 11
Success Awaits You

And you shall remember the Lord your God, for it is He who gives you power to get wealth, that He may establish His covenant which He swore to your fathers, as it is this day. (Deuteronomy 8:18).

You were not born to die; you were born to overcome death. You were not born to be poor, you were born to overcome poverty. The potential to do this is built into your DNA. Your humble beginnings is irrelevant to who you are becoming. Forget the things that are behind you (good and bad) and press towards the mark of the higher calling on your life. God is taking you somewhere you have never been before. Where you are is a pinned location on your journey, not the destination.

What does success look like to you? Whatever it is, you can achieve it. It may seem impossible, but the God who lives in you says "We can do this." You got this! Failures are steps upward. Mistakes are lessons to grow from. God can part the sea for you to get to the other side, or He will make you walk on water as if it is solid ground. Any wall erected to suppress your potential can fall with a shout. God's dream for you is out of this world, and if He needs to give you wings to get you there, He will. Success is your portion. You are not a failure.

Day 12
You Are Loved

Just as He chose us in Him before the foundation of the world, that we should be holy and without blame before Him in love. (Ephesians 1:4).

Before the world was created, God chose you. He loved you ages before you were a seed in your mother's womb. It means the very thought of you in God's mind made you real long before you got here. Remember, God lives outside of time, space and matter. These three exist in God, not independent of God. This is why God can have an "expected end" for you, and He knows the path you need to take to get there. You must see that you are eternally loved, even in the midst of your process. God has not abandoned you. He walks with you.

Though you were born into this world a sinner, God took on the full responsibility to save you and cloth you in His righteousness. Your clothes are new. Your mind is being renewed. You are a new creation. The world has never seen another like you and waits with bated breath and deep groanings for the fullness of who you are to manifest. This is true love; that vile creatures like fallen humanity can be chosen for a divine purpose. God's love for you is without conditions. You are accepted in the beloved.

Day 13
Don't Be Afraid to Start

For who has despised the day of small things? For these seven rejoice to see the plumb line in the hand of Zerubbabel. They are the eyes of the Lord, which scan to and fro throughout the whole earth. (Zechariah 4:10).

Sometimes we want to start at the end. We can see where we want to go, but we don't want to take the painstaking journey to get there, so we keep an image of the end as our starting point, and it is too much, so we never start. The resources may not be there to start there. The only way to embark on such a journey is to start from where you are. Don't expand the dream so big that you cannot find what you need to start. The end goal must always be there, but it cannot be the starting point. Be patient with the process and take it one step at a time.

If you stand on one end of the road and look at a location at the opposite end, you will not get there unless you begin to take the necessary steps. You may not know the challenges that are ahead, and anxiety and fear may project images in your mind of worse-case scenarios and chaotic encounters, but if you allow that to stop you, you will never know what is waiting for you at the end. Fear can be a deterrent on our journey, but it can also become an ally. It's a matter of perspective. Fear is described as False Evidence Appearing Real. Faith says, "Go for it anyway." Do it afraid.

Day 14
Find Help to Finish Strong

Though one may be overpowered by another, two can withstand him. And a threefold cord is not quickly broken. (Ecclesiastes 4:12).

There is power in agreement. You cannot do it alone. You were never meant to do it alone. God said it is not good for a man to be alone. This is not just about companionship. There is great power in agreement. Jesus says if two agree, it will be done. This is a guarantee that accompanies agreement, so don't be afraid to partner with others in getting it done. You have great things to do, and you will need others who can align with your vision. There are people whose purpose is tied to yours.

Be open to collaboration. It doesn't mean you join with everyone who wants to attach themselves to you. It does mean that you must be discerning to know when God is aligning you with others who can help you. Everyone carries something unique, but we are all connected to one another because the same God lives in those who believe. Jesus discipled His followers, then sent them out two by two. Why didn't He send each man on his own mission? I hear people refer to these divine connections as "destiny helpers." Whatever you want to call them, God will position people in your life who will help you to finish strong.

Day 15
Giving Empowers You

Give, and it will be given to you: good measure, pressed down, shaken together, and running over will be put into your bosom. For with the same measure that you use, it will be measured back to you. (Luke 6:38).

You can determine how blessed you are by the measure you use when giving of yourself. This is a divine law: Give and it will be given to you. It means you are not reducing your resources by giving, but increasing it and opening up the possibility for an immeasurable release into your life. You empower yourself by giving, not by holding back. What you try to keep for yourself is an uninitiated blessing. In order to receive, you must be willing to release.

God so loved the world that He <u>gave</u> His only Son. In giving His most treasured gift to an undeserving world, He received an eternal family of sons and daughters. This is the principle God wants you to get. Jesus says if you try to hold on to your life, you will lose it. But if you are willing to release even that, then you will find it. Giving is love, and love empowers you to walk in uncommon favour. That thing you think you cannot live without, be willing to release it and it will come back to you as something better. Give the ground a seed and it will give you a fruit tree that can feed an entire community.

Day 16
Be Diligent at Work

And whatever you do, do it heartily, as to the Lord and not to men. (Colossians 3:23).

Perspective is very important in your walk of faith. It is important how you see and where your focus is. You may not like your job or the people you have to work with, but you have a job. You have the means to provide for yourself and your family. You could be jobless. In most cases, it was God who made it even possible for you to get that job. Be thankful for what you have and work as if God was the one who employed you. He sees everything that you are doing.

Promotion comes from God. He is also a rewarder of good works. He says no good thing with He withhold from you. Trust His promises. He knows when you are ready to receive a higher position, and He will make it happen. Enter the age of peace and rest and work with diligence. Go above and beyond. Exceed the expectations of those you work for and work with. Go that extra mile. Your reward is sure so whatever you do, do it as unto the Lord.

Day 17
Unlimited Grace

Moreover the law entered that the offense might abound. But where sin abounded, grace abounded much more. (Romans 5:20).

Grace is unmerited favour. It is not a license to sin but actually empowers us to live free from sin. Grace is always available to you. It was God's idea. No man can measure the level of grace you receive or control its disbursement. God does that. Sin is not greater than grace. God does not condemn those who are in Christ. He knows we are weak and prone to failure. He is the remedy. He is the cure. Feed on Him. Focus on Him and all will be well.

The journey of life is filled with many detours. Sin is alluring, and we are sometimes pulled away from our course by it. We fall, we fail, we mess up, and our God-given garment of righteousness becomes smeared in the mud puddles of our failure. If we go to God every time, He purges our garments, gives us a new heart, and renews our spirit so we can continue our journey. That is unlimited grace, and it is your birthright as a child of God.

Day 18
Live Well

Beloved, I pray that you may prosper in all things and be in health, just as your soul prospers. (3 John 1:2).

It is God's desire that we prosper and be in good health as our soul prospers. Jesus exemplified this reality by healing all those who came to Him and granted them wholeness. God's will is not for us to live fragmented, poor, and sick. Jesus overcame, and He has empowered us to do the same. Our present realities are not the final discourse of our lives. Your greater days are still ahead of you. Keep hope and faith alive. A new season is coming.

Live well. Eat healthy. Move your body. Join a gym—do three days a week. Don't overdo it. Set a pace that you can maintain overtime. Avoid processed food as it damages the temple of God overtime. Grow your own food. Plant a tree and help the world be a better place. Do not contribute to its pollution and destruction. Live consciously that this is the world God made for us and gave us the responsibility to care for it as we care for our bodies. We have the power to change our lives, change the lives of others, and make this world a better place for the next generation we take into this world.

Leave the world better than how you found it when you came.

Day 19
Arise From the Dust

Shake yourself from the dust, arise; Sit down, O Jerusalem! Loose yourself from the bonds of your neck, O captive daughter of Zion! (Isaiah 52:2).

Shut down the drama in your life. It is unhealthy. Conflict will always exist between different personalities, but that is what makes us unique. We are all different. Arguing and fighting creates disease and profits nothing. Do your best to stay away from negative, selfish, energy-draining relationships that do not honor you, or even worse, use you, abuse you and take advantage of your kindness.

Don't buy into their negativity or guilt trips. Resolve to live in peace. Don't attempt to change others. There is enough work to do on yourself. Recognize the power that is in unity. We will accomplish very little being divided. We must work together so develop relationships where all parties can grow and create an atmosphere of mutual respect, love, and appreciation.

Free yourself from inner chaos through meditation, relaxation, and stillness. It is in those quiet moments that God will speak into your spirit and reveal His heart. What you create inside of yourself will manifest outside yourself. God deposited His glory and kingdom inside you. Create a sanctuary where you can live in peace, relax your mind, revive your spirit, and renew your purpose.

Day 20
Walk Worthy of the Call

I, therefore, the prisoner of the Lord, beseech you to walk worthy of the calling with which you were called. (Ephesians 4:1).

Not everyone will feel the same about the effort you make in achieving something. We desire differently in life. The fact is, we get what we feel worthy of having. Feeling worthy helps you move along in life. The reality is, if you don't feel worthy of accomplishing what you want, it slows down your progress in life.

Many set goals and then feel unworthy to pursue them. They are locked in the "I'm not good enough" and "I am not worthy of this" mentality, which limits and restrict their efforts. They don't push hard enough because they don't think they deserve it, and every setback or mishap is seen as a sign to stop pressing forward. Be encouraged to set your goals, feel worthy of these goals, and live to achieve them. Never be contented pursuing your dreams until they become a reality, and never stop pursuing or you will not achieve them.

Day 21
Keep Pressing

I press toward the goal for the prize of the upward call of God in Christ Jesus. (Philippians 3:14).

There will always be more reasons to stop than move forward, and this applies to every stratosphere of life. Obstacles come to hinder, stop, delay, or block our progress. We are often derailed or thrown off course by unexpected circumstances that may appear like a sudden windstorm. Very often it is our divine purpose that gets shelved for more mundane tasks. But on the hardest of journeys, up the mountainside, every climber knows you can't focus too far ahead, but every step counts for that is the way to get to your desired destination; one step at a time. Every step is one step away from where you have been and one step closer to where you are going.

If you keep pressing forward, you must get to your destination. It is a law of nature established by the Creator that cannot be modified, changed, or revised. It really doesn't matter how far you are going, if you keep moving in the desired direction, you will eventually get there. The laws of God always work in your favour.

Day 22
Live Without Fear

For God has not given us a spirit of fear, but of power and of love and of a sound mind. (2 Timothy 1:7).

Fear has the power to stop you in your tracks, and hinder you from progressing, developing and moving forward. It has the capacity to prevent your vision from ever becoming a reality, but you have the power to overcome fear because God lives in you. Greater is the one who abides in you than they that are in the world.

What is inside you is greater than what is on the outside, and fear lives outside you. It desires to have you, to take up residence in you, but you have what it takes to live beyond your fears. Don't let what you are afraid of stop you from doing what you are called to do. Use fear to confirm your calling. Fear will always challenge what God has told you to do. Do it anyway. Courage is not you operating in the absence of fear, but choosing to live, move and exist despite the presence of fear. It is knowing that the Goliaths in your life may destroy you but running towards it anyway. God will give you the victory.

Day 23
Come Out From Among Them

Therefore "Come out from among them and be separate, says the Lord. Do not touch what is unclean, and I will receive you." (2 Corinthians 6:17).

Negative relationships can be toxic to your spiritual life. There is an age-old saying, "Show me your friends and I will tell you who you are." God is the one who truly defines us, but if you hang around negativity and contempt, it will breed negativity and contempt in your own life. You become the environment you associate yourself with. You hold on to what you think you need, but sometimes God is trying to rescue you from that which is destroying you.

A good tree will always produce good fruit, but it will only take one bad apple to spoil the whole bunch. You must release negative relationships in order to embrace what God has for you. Not everyone in your life was put there by God. When the farmer sowed seeds of wheat, the enemy came in and sowed tares among them. Learn to recognize those relationships that will make you better, and let go of those that don't.

Day 24
Nurse Your Dream

"While the earth remains, seedtime and harvest, cold and heat, winter and summer, and day and night shall not cease." (Genesis 8:22).

When planted, the Chinese bamboo shows no sign of growth on the surface for up to four years. Eventually, when a stem breaks out on the surface, in a very short time the tree grows exponentially, up to 98 inches in 24 hours. Keep planting, keep sowing, and keep gleaning your field, even if there is no indication that there is going to be a harvest. Be assured that the season of harvest will come. When it does, it will be quick and abundant.

Every seed you sow will bring a harvest. It is a spiritual law that never fails. There is no seed that you have planted that will be wasted. God is just, and He rewards those who obey His principles. If you sow, you will reap. If you are not reaping, then it simply means you are not sowing. Your dream is your responsibility. There is no way it will come to fruition without you, so keep nursing your dream.

Day 25
Shake Off Mediocrity

But you are a chosen generation, a royal priesthood, a holy nation, His own special people, that you may proclaim the praises of Him who called you out of darkness into His marvelous light. (1 Peter 2:9).

You are a child of the King, not a king, but the King. There is nothing normal about you. You are counted among royalty. It is in your blood. Mediocrity should not be named among you, but seek to do all things with excellence and integrity.

You represent heaven, and heaven supports what you do, so do it with dignity. Your best is yet to come, but you must press into it. As an heir of God's kingdom, your future is infinitely better than your present and past. Whatever your heart finds to do, do it well and with all your heart. This pleases the Father. Do not strive as if you are striving for man but work as if you are labouring for God. When God gives gifts, He gives the best. As you give Him service in your day-to-day lives, do it with all your heart.

Day 26
The King's Domain

Do you see a man who excels in his work? He will stand before kings; He will not stand before unknown men. (Proverbs 22:29).

Whatever you are given to do, do it with all your heart and strength. Work as if you are working for God, and not for men. You will be noticed, you will be honoured, and you will be exalted. Those who humble themselves will always be lifted up.

Stop complaining that the task is too great. You are empowered to do all things through Christ who gives you strength. Be a good steward of your time, talents, and resources, and in time you will be called upon to sit at the King's Table. Have you seen a man diligent in his work? Show me that man, and I will show you a man who will one day sit at the King's Table. There is a promotion waiting for you. There is a seat at the King's table with your name on it. No one can occupy that place but you.

Day 27
Live Life With Excitement

For in Him we live and move and have our being, as also some of your own poets have said, 'For we are also His offspring.' (Acts 17:28).

You were born to live in the presence and glory of God. As fish was made to live in the sea, animals and plants on land, birds in the air, our natural habitat is the glory of God. When we sin, we fall short of that glory. But Jesus has restored and is restoring all things.

Like Adam, we are privileged to have God come down in the cool of the day to commune with us. We are also seated with Him in heaven where we commune with Him. Make time for Him; make room for Him.

In Him is a life free from limitations and fear. In Him we truly live and breath. He makes living on earth a very exciting journey.

Day 28
Always Pursue Excellence

And this I pray, that your love may abound still more and more in knowledge and all discernment, that you may approve the things that are excellent, that you may be sincere and without offense till the day of Christ. (Philippians 1:9-10).

God wants you to abound and to excel in both your inward character, and also what you do, i.e., good deeds and behaviour. In this way you are loving God with all your heart. So, pursue excellence. This should be a goal and will confirm your spiritual maturity.

Excellence must be motivated by your values, motives, and priorities. Never give up. Don't allow your heart to be troubled to the point of becoming inactive and passive. Keep moving towards your success and do your very best. You have what it takes to be even better than you think you are.

Day 29
Keep Getting Up

For a righteous man may fall seven times and rise again, but the wicked shall fall by calamity. (Proverbs 24:16).

Setbacks will come, but it is your response that is paramount to your life. Great men and women of the Bible have suffered great persecutions for no other reason but that they were living for God. No one promised that when we come to God, everything will be perfect. It is through hardship that we learn to stand.

In the same way a baby will fall multiple times before learning to walk, you will fall multiple times as you learn to walk in the Spirit. It is a part of the process, so embrace the process. Everyone desires to get to the palace without going through the 'prison.' Through your trials, you will grow to become more than a conqueror, so embrace the tough times. Accept the process. When you fall, get up and keep getting up. You will come out victorious on the other side.

Day 30
Go The Extra Mile

And whoever compels you to go one mile, go with him two. (Matthew 5:41).

The extra-mile principle propels you beyond your human limitations. It is then that the power of God will manifest in your life. It is a work of the Spirit for you to make that effort to go the extra mile. It speaks to the strength that is within you.

You are more than you think, and you have access to more than you can imagine. There is a God living in you—the one true living God. Remove the limitations you have put on God by putting them on yourself. You are not weak or inadequate. When your own strength fails, draw on the joy of the Lord and that will give you the strength to go further.

Day 31
Live With Boldness

The wicked flee when no one pursues, but the righteous are bold as a lion. (Proverbs 28:1).

If the God who creates all and is in all and is the source of all existence lives inside you, why are you afraid? What is there to fear? Is there one who is greater than God? If God is greater, then what do you fear?

Among the wheat of courage planted in you, the enemy has sown tares of fear. From which perspective will you live? You have the capacity to be bold, so perfect love can liberate you from all your fears. Live in the boldness that you already possess. Be bold enough to do what God has called you to do. True courage is running towards your giants, even in the presence of fear itself.

If God is a God of the impossible, He will always ask you to do what you think you are incapable of doing. Fear will try everything in its power to stop you from manifesting that which God wants to birth in and through you. Choose to be bold, even in the face of fear, and you will be surprised at what you can accomplish.

Day 32
Take The Leap

So He said, "Come." And when Peter had come down out of the boat, he walked on the water to go to Jesus. (Matthew 14:29).

When Jesus says "Come," it is an invitation to all, but only a few ever respond. Every step you take in life is a step of faith. Every project you embark upon is done from a place of faith. Every new job you take or challenge you face is from a place of faith. We don't always know the outcome of anything we take on, but we do it anyway.

When Peter stepped off that boat, the only assurance he had was that Jesus was standing on the water. The mentality then is that if Jesus could do it, so can I. The Master is calling you out into the deep. Take that leap. Take that step. There is only one sure way to get to your destiny, and that is one step at a time—one giant leap at a time. The thought does count, but only an act of the will can get you there.

Day 33
Raise The Bar Higher

And whatever you do in word or deed, do all in the name of the Lord Jesus, giving thanks to God the Father through Him. (Colossians 3:17).

Why limit yourself when the limitless One lives inside you?

Remove the limitations, take away the barriers; you are a child of the King. He owns it all, and there is nothing that escapes His influence. You belong to Him, adopted into His family. What is His also belongs to you. As Jesus is, so are you on this earth. His power dwells in you to do and accomplish all things, so lift the bar a little higher. Challenge yourself to attempt what many may think is impossible. Go for it.

Challenges and obstacles are not a reason to turn away and give up. Too many people give up just moments before getting their breakthrough. Don't let that be you. If you don't press through everything that seeks to stop you from achieving greatness, you will never experience what is on the other side. The strength you need to go on is within you, and only those who never give up can change the world.

Day 34
Invest in Your Dream

For this reason I also suffer these things; nevertheless I am not ashamed, for I know whom I have believed and am persuaded that He is able to keep what I have committed to Him until that Day. (2 Timothy 1:12).

God has a plan for your life. He has dreams for you. There is a scroll existing with your name on it. Recorded on that scroll is everything you were meant to accomplish, every dream you were meant to realize. It may cost you, but the value of your dream far outweighs the sacrifice you put in to make it happen. Invest in your dream.

Don't devalue your worth or limit the potential of your destiny. You were sent to earth to do great things. Seek to fulfill the dream your Father has for you. Great things are produced through great sacrifice, so know your value and be willing to invest in that dream.

Day 35
Stop Complaining

Do all things without complaining and disputing, that you may become blameless and harmless, children of God without fault in the midst of a crooked and perverse generation, among whom you shine as lights in the world. (Philippians 2:14-15).

You are light. Your life illuminates in a dark place, like a candle in a dark room. Complaining clouds your light, pulls a veil over it, and obscures your influence. Stop complaining. You have power in your mouth to move, shift and change your reality.

Complaining is agreeing with the enemy and what he is trying to accomplish. Stop speaking death and start to speak life. Speak life over your family, community, household, workplace, and church. There is great power in your tongue, so use it for good.

Day 36
Speak Up When Necessary

Death and life are in the power of the tongue, and those who love it will eat its fruit. (Proverbs 18:21).

Stephen spoke and they stoned him to death. Paul spoke and he was beaten almost to death. Peter spoke and he was thrown into prison. In the natural it might not seem worth it to speak up but look at the fruit it produced. Two thousand years later, we are living off the words that Paul, Peter, and Stephen spoke. Their words have born even greater fruit than they could have imagined. What if they had not said anything?

Your words are being recorded in heaven, so speak life. Speak health. Speak prosperity. Speak against the plans and schemes of the enemy. Speak the truth, despite the consequences. Your words have the potential to bear much fruit. Use the power of your tongue to frame the reality you want to experience. Do not contribute to the "noise" in the world, but speak from that place where you are seated with Christ and watch heaven begin to invade earth.

Day 37
You Sow What You Reap

Do not be deceived, God is not mocked; for whatever a man sows, that he will also reap. (Galatians 6:7).

There is no seed that you plant in the ground that will not produce a great harvest. You may not be able to reap immediately, but you will. It is a spiritual principle or law established by Jehovah God. What you sow, you will also reap. The more you sow, is the more you will reap. This is not just talking about money but your time, intellect, resources, etc.

Don't hold back. Don't allow yourself to be stingy. Give from what you have been blessed with. Do not just give to be blessed or to receive. Give because you are blessed, and you will receive. As your life came from a seed, everything you produce will also come from a seed. The potential you have within you is given to you as a seed that must be planted and nurtured into the fruit-bearing tree it was meant to be.

Day 38
Follow Positive Examples

Imitate me, just as I also imitate Christ. (I Corinthians 11:1).

If you keep doing what you always do, don't expect any different results. If your desire is to have new experiences, then do something different. Observe what works for others and copy the good that good people do. You will see better results.

Don't limit yourself to what you have been taught growing up. There is a vast, unexplored field of knowledge and opportunities ahead of you just waiting to be discovered. Don't be afraid to make mistakes. Don't define who you are by your failures. Every failure is a steppingstone to go higher. Stay positive and challenge yourself to be even greater and do more than you could ever imagine.

Day 39
I Can Do It

I can do all things through Christ who strengthens me. (Philippians 4:13).

If God says you can, who can convince you that you can't? Believe what God says about you. Believe what He says you can do. He is not kidding.

What is it that you have a desire to accomplish? Does it seem impossible? Believe in yourself and who you are in Christ Jesus. You are not the same person you used to be. All things have become new, so don't be afraid to try new things. Try impossible things. Face your fears. Run towards that challenge full throttle. See every challenge as an opportunity to grow in faith. Faith untested is no faith at all, so press beyond the limits of your own mind. Tell yourself that you can and you will, and let nothing stop you.

Day 40
Let Not Your Heart Be Troubled

Let not your heart be troubled; you believe in God, believe also in Me. (John 14:1).

Someone once said, "Live from your heart and not from your brain." Your heart knows the truth. When your soul is downcast, pick yourself up. Encourage yourself, speak over yourself. Depression can only linger in the darkness of silence, but when you speak up and speak out, darkness dissipates. There is power in your words.

"Let not your heart be troubled" denotes a choice that we have the power to make. It was King David who spoke to his depressed soul, "Why are you cast down, oh my soul? Hope thou in God." (see Psalm 42:5). Your hope is not in this world or the things of this world. You have an eternal hope in a land that will never deteriorate or waste away. Your hope is in eternity.

Day 41
Be Anxious For Nothing

Be anxious for nothing, but in everything by prayer and supplication, with thanksgiving, let your requests be made known to God; and the peace of God, which surpasses all understanding, will guard your hearts and minds through Christ Jesus. (Philippians 4:6-7).

Expectation is the essence of manifestation. To receive, you must first expect. The opposing emotion would be anxiety. Anxiety is expecting the negative to happen. Anxiety will manifest the wrong reality. Expectation is desiring what God has promised. Be eager, not anxious.

Be anxious for nothing, but with prayer and supplication, let your request be made known to God. When you submit your request, rest in the fact that God has heard and will answer. He promised He will. Don't allow your mind to be flooded with doubts but live at that place of expectation and watch God move. There are opposing voices that will try to convince us that God will not act. Do not believe them. Believe God and stand on His promises with eagerness.

Day 42
Be Unique

Now you are the body of Christ, and members individually. (1 Corinthians 12:27).

You were made for a purpose. Within your DNA is a unique divine destiny just for you. There is something particular that you are called to do. That is your assignment, but you must work cohesively with others. We have often heard that if you don't take your place, someone else will. If this is true, then why didn't God choose someone else when Jonah said no?

You are a part of the body of Christ. As a member, you have your unique function. Don't try to do it like others but do it like you. Be you. Be unique, and indispensable. Do not be puffed up. Humble yourself, and you will be exalted.

Day 43
Don't Succumb to Peer Pressure

But you are a chosen generation, a royal priesthood, a holy nation, His own special people, that you may proclaim the praises of Him who called you out of darkness into His marvelous light. (1 Peter 2:9).

You don't have to do what those around you are doing. You were made to stand out, not to fit in. Quit trying to fit in with the crowd. You are in this world but not of this world. You are special, royalty, a rare commodity.

There is nothing regular or normal about you, so dare to be different. Dare to set new trends and change the culture. Dare to challenge the status quo of fashion and how you represent or conduct yourself in this world. Be different. Be unique. You are called to represent God before men and not to be influenced by the latest fad.

Day 44
Be An Eagle

But those who wait on the Lord shall renew their strength; They shall mount up with wings like eagles, they shall run and not be weary, they shall walk and not faint. (Isaiah 40:31).

God's mercy is new for you every morning. Leave yesterday's challenges and failures where they belong. There is fresh bread available in your eternal basket every day. You do not need to leave any for tomorrow. Every day will provide something new for itself.

Be like an eagle who soars with very little effort. Let the wind of God's presence carry you wherever God's will is. He will fold Himself under your wing and carry you, but only if you let Him. An eagle doesn't worry about falling or crashing. They know that what carries them is sufficient for the journey.

Eagles fly from a place of rest. They don't exert too much energy. Even in flight, their strength is renewed. Be like an eagle.

Day 45
Get Up and Get Going

I press toward the goal for the prize of the upward call of God in Christ Jesus. (Philippians 3:14).

When you are overwhelmed by challenges, stop long enough to count your blessings. You will be surprised at all that the Lord has done. You may be experiencing pain in your feet, but you are blessed to have feet. You may be moving slower than you used to, but you are blessed because you are moving. You may not have enough money to clear your bills for the month, but you have a job, you have life, you have the strength and ability to earn.

Things won't always go right, but it could always be worse. If you look hard enough, for each day, you can find reasons to get up and keep going. Fake it until you make it if you have to. There is no shame in that. If you were not resilient, you would not have been conceived. Learn from that and keep going. You are not there yet.

Day 46
Live In Gratitude

Enter into His gates with thanksgiving, and into His courts with praise. Be thankful to Him, and bless His name. (Psalm 100:4).

Be thankful in all circumstances. You will not always get it the way you want. Things will not always work out according to plan but be grateful. Give thanks for what you do have, and don't allow yourself to be consumed with depression for what you do not have.

Those who learn to be content with what they do have qualify to receive more. No matter what you are facing today, you have life. You belong to God, and nothing you are experiencing right now has caught your Heavenly Father off-guard. He knows the way that you take, so give thanks that despite everything, you still have life, and where there is life, there is hope.

Day 47
Live Full, Die Empty

For You formed my inward parts; You covered me in my mother's womb. I will praise You, for I am fearfully and wonderfully made; marvelous are Your works, and that my soul knows very well. My frame was not hidden from You, when I was made in secret, and skillfully wrought in the lowest parts of the earth. Your eyes saw my substance, being yet unformed. And in Your book they all were written, the days fashioned for me, when as yet there were none of them. (Psalm 139:13-16).

Whatever you receive, give. It keeps the cycle of life going. Be a stream, not a well. A well retains what is put inside it, unless someone deliberately goes and pulls from it. A stream releases immediately what goes into it. You were called to be an everflowing stream, not a well. What you retain will grow stagnant, but when you release it, you keep making room for more.

Live life to the fullest, but seek to die empty. Those are the words of world-renowned motivational speaker Myles Munroe. The purpose of receiving is not to retain but to release. The Apostles were told, "Freely you have received, freely you should give." (see Matthew 10:8). Keep nothing for yourself. You won't be able to take it with you.

Day 48
This Came To Pass

For our light affliction, which is but for a moment, is working for us a far more exceeding and eternal weight of glory, while we do not look at the things which are seen, but at the things which are not seen. For the things which are seen are temporary, but the things which are not seen are eternal. (2 Corinthians 4:17-18).

Storms are temporary. They will not last always. It doesn't matter how fierce they are or how much damage they are capable of inflicting, they must eventually pass. What God has in store for you is better than what you have now. He has a future reserved for you that is infinitely better than your present and past. He desires to reveal His glory in and through you.

In the midst of the storm, He wants you to know that you may not be instantly delivered from it, but He is with you. He will take you through it. If God takes you to it, He can take you through it. Rest in the confidence of knowing that you are not alone, and this too will pass.

Day 49
Have a Winning Mindset

If indeed you have heard Him and have been taught by Him, as the truth is in Jesus: that you put off, concerning your former conduct, the old man which grows corrupt according to the deceitful lusts, and be renewed in the spirit of your mind. (Ephesians 4:21-23).

It can be hard to think like a winner in the midst of losing. We fail from time to time and for various reasons, and very often we get knocked down. Those things will happen, but what is really important is how you respond to it.

While in prison, Paul wrote a letter to the church stating how free he was. His thought-life reflected a kingdom reality that far surpasses our present state. It doesn't matter what you are going through right now, it is the mindset you maintain that will determine how victorious you will be. Before you can win, you must see yourself as a winner against all odds.

Day 50
Take the Lead

In all things showing yourself to be a pattern of good works; in doctrine showing integrity, reverence, incorruptibility, sound speech that cannot be condemned, that one who is an opponent may be ashamed, having nothing evil to say of you. (Titus 2:7-8).

Your purpose is to keep moving forward. There are obstacles and challenges that are designed specifically to stop you from moving. It is easy to be passive and rendered inactive, but you were pre-destined to ride on and take the lead. You were created to lead, to set new trends, change culture, and influence society.

You are a beacon of light set on top of a hill to help illuminate those who are around you. Be a light to their path, a source of encouragement, a beacon of hope, a fountain of love to those who come in contact with you. Those who know you, must know Christ, so do not be afraid to take the lead and ride on. Be an example of who God is in everything that you do; in your action and speech, let your light shine.

Day 51
Remove the Lid From the Jar

But we have this treasure in earthen vessels, that the excellence of the power may be of God and not of us. (2 Corinthians 4:7).

God has put greatness in you. Within your body, you carry a heavenly treasure that God has entrusted you with. Be determined to be a good steward of what God has placed inside you. Open the jar of your life, and release the glory of God on the earth.

As the waters cover the sea, the earth will be covered with the knowledge of the glory of God that you carry inside you. Don't resist or fight the urge to be different, to do things differently, to take on challenges that others shy away from. There is nothing impossible for the God who lives inside you, so stop putting limits on yourself. You can do it. God says you can. Dare to believe what He says, and walk the path that He has laid out for you, even before the foundations of the earth were set.

Day 52
Don't Be a Grasshopper

There we saw the giants (the descendants of Anak came from the giants); and we were like grasshoppers in our own sight, and so we were in their sight. (Numbers 13:33).

There is no situation that is bigger than God. There is no enemy who can stand against God. He is, was, and will always be. Change how you think. Renew your mind. Assume new thoughts. God's thoughts for you are higher than yours; His ways greater. Start to think big.

You may seem like a grasshopper to your enemy, but in God's eyes you are more than a conqueror. He has already given you the victory. He will teach you to win wars without fighting. You can praise your way around all your Jericho walls and watch them fall. Your sword is in your mouth, so declare who you are and who Your God is to all who oppose you.

Goliath was never a match for David. Goliath died without knowing that. It is not what your enemy thinks about you that matters. It is what you think about yourself, so believe what God says about you and walk in that. You are not a grasshopper unless you choose to be.

Day 53
No One Needs to Approve Your Dream

Now to Him who is able to do exceedingly abundantly above all that we ask or think, according to the power that works in us. (Ephesians 3:20).

Do not be intimidated by how impossible your dream may look. Be motivated to press toward your dream, even if you feel alone. There are some people who will only seek to kill your dream. Don't let them.

Do not be moved by the seeds of doubt and discouragement that people may sow. God gives dreams pre-approved. You don't need anyone to approve it. Whatever God lays on your heart to do, do it with all the boldness you have. Pull on all the resources He has connected you with. God will always supply what you need to fulfil your dream.

Day 54
A Day Called Tomorrow

Don't put it off; do it now! Don't rest until you do. (Proverbs 6:4 - NLT).

Why do you keep putting off for tomorrow what you can do today? There will always be a tomorrow. Today is the gift you are given each morning. Tomorrow is never for you, so don't move your todays into tomorrow. You procrastinate because tomorrow never comes.

Every new day is the eve of a new tomorrow. What you plan to do tomorrow may never get done. Seek to do it today. You are charged to be a good steward of your time. Time is not something you get but something you make. Make time for what is important. Make time for what matters. Live in your todays and give no thought to your tomorrows. Tomorrow will provide for itself. God is a God of today. Tomorrow is a fantasy.

Stop procrastination and take control of your time. Schedule properly, prioritize well, and learn to say no.

Day 55
Today is the Day

Go to the ant, you sluggard! Consider her ways and be wise, which, having no captain, overseer or ruler, provides her supplies in the summer, and gathers her food in the harvest. (Proverbs 6:6-8).

Today is the only day you have. Tomorrow is not promised. Yesterday is gone. Live today as if this is the only day you have to live. Maximize on the moments that will present themselves to you today and stay alert for any new doors of opportunity that may open to you.

There will be challenges and hurdles to cross, but every challenge is an opportunity to become better. Face your day with a smile. Confuse the enemy. He hates when you smile under pressure. Give praise consistently, especially when you are tempted to do otherwise. The one who learns to praise God under pressure, learns to live and walk in victory. Today is your day of victory.

Day 56
Fight the Good Fight

I have fought the good fight, I have finished the race, I have kept the faith. (2 Timothy 4:7).

There is a winning streak in your blood. You were designed to conquer giants and take back land that is rightfully your inheritance. You have a very rich inheritance embedded in your DNA.

When Jesus said 'It is finished,' there was a completeness that took place in the spirit. All that you need was already paid for by Jesus. You need only to conquer and possess. You have everything you need to win. You are backed by heaven. God is on your side. He believes in you. He has made all the resources of heaven available to you. He is pressing you forward to become all He has designed you to be. Move forward in the power of the Spirit. You cannot lose. You will not be defeated. God will be a wall of fire around you and the glory within you. That is all it takes to win.

Day 57
Take Charge

Here is the patience of the saints; here are those who keep the commandments of God and the faith of Jesus. (Revelation 14:12).

Be proactive and not passive. Those who remain passive accomplish very little. There is a saying that you must 'take the bull by the horn.' This speaks about making it happen, as opposed to waiting for it to happen.

You have the Holy Spirit living inside you. You have all the power you need to take charge. Take charge of your family. Take charge of your homes, workplaces, and community. Take charge of your health and wellbeing. Stop feeling sorry for yourself, and just get up and do something about it. A soldier at war knows that he must always be ready to take action. There is more in store for you than what you have now. God has more for you, but you must take action; you must make it happen. Whatever you desire, you can have. You see it because it already belongs to you.

Day 58
Wake Up, Giant

So he answered and said to me: "This is the word of the Lord to Zerubbabel: 'Not by might nor by power, but by My Spirit,' Says the Lord of hosts." (Zechariah 4:6).

Can a man place limits on God? If the answer is no, and this same God lives in you, can a man put limits on you? You are much bigger than the one you stare at in the mirror. There is a giant in you just waiting to be awakened from slumber.

You are not just a giant but a giant slayer. There are many giants in the world today. Giants of fear, worry, anxiety, pornography, fornication, and drugs. God has called and equipped you to take these giants down. You have the power inside you.

David was much smaller than Goliath, but that was not his confession. David knew his God and recognized the difference in power and stature. David knew who he was in the eyes of the Lord. He was no grasshopper. When you challenge the giants in your life, God will fight for you. With God fighting for you, you cannot lose.

Day 59
First Things First

But seek first the kingdom of God and His righteousness, and all these things shall be added to you. (Matthew 6:33).

Don't just seek the gifts but seek after the Giver. Don't just pursue healing but pursue the Healer. We must prioritize God above all things. It is easy to put things and people above God, but this never pleases Him. He desires to be first, and first thing is first. God wants to reveal His heart to you, but you must take the time to listen, to sit at His feet.

Mary and Martha are sisters with different personalities. One was sitting at Jesus' feet, and the other was busy making preparations. Mary was commended as having chosen the better thing, and that will not be taken away from her. There is a place you can be where nothing can move you, and nothing can touch you. There is a place in God where the enemy cannot touch you. Seek first the kingdom of God and His righteousness and you will lack nothing.

Day 60
Take Responsibility

Confess your trespasses to one another, and pray for one another, that you may be healed. The effective, fervent prayer of a righteous man avails much. (James 5:16).

You have heard it said many times, "No one is perfect." Maybe you have even said it. While this is true, never make the mistake of relinquishing responsibility for your actions. You alone are responsible for what you do, and you alone will stand to give an account, so take responsibility and be accountable to someone.

Everyone needs a mentor. There is always someone who has already gone through what you are experiencing and has walked away more than a conqueror. You can learn from them. You can be inspired and motivated by them. Never allow yourself to be mentored by someone on your level. You must take responsibility for who you allow to mentor you. We are all prone to make mistakes and sin from time to time. Recognize that your sin is paid for, and go to God. Don't run away from God. Adam ran to hide after he sinned. God went looking for him. God comes looking for you when you sin. He wants to cleanse you and make you new. That is just the kind of Father He is.

Day 61
Servants on Horses

Folly is set in great dignity, while the rich sit in a lowly place. I have seen servants on horses, while princes walk on the ground like servants. He who digs a pit will fall into it, and whoever breaks through a wall will be bitten by a serpent. (Ecclesiastes 10:6-8).

Jabez had discovered a grave error in his own life. 1 Chronicles 4:9-10 says, "Now Jabez was more honorable than his brothers, and his mother called his name Jabez, saying, "Because I bore him in pain." And Jabez called on the God of Israel saying, "Oh, that You would bless me indeed, and enlarge my territory, that Your hand would be with me, and that You would keep me from evil, that I may not cause pain!" So God granted him what he requested." God granted his request.

Jabez chose to pray instead of complain about his unfortunate situation, and God turned it around. He wants to turn your mess into a message; your test into a testimony. It doesn't matter where you are from, or your seemingly humble beginnings, social status or the class you fall in, God can put servants on horses and princes to walk the ground like a slave. He can flip the script.

He can enlarge your area of influence. You are already blessed beyond measure.

Day 62
Feeling Out of Breath

By the word of the Lord the heavens were made, and all the host of them by the breath of His mouth. (Psalm 33:6).

Every winner knows that there are times we will feel out of breath. It is at that moment we are prompted to stop and 'catch our breath.' There is nothing wrong with taking a well-needed break in the race of life. We can be so consumed in the rat race that we just keep on going until our bodies send a powerful signal for us to slow down, and for some of us that means a rest stop in a hospital bed. Regardless of how busy you are chasing dreams, making the impossible real and living the life, you must seek to create that balance where every now and again you stop for a breather.

Take a walk along the beach. Sit with a loved one and watch the sun come up or go down. Go on a movie date, a trip to the zoo, a safari, or take a few days cruise on the sea. Take some time to travel to another country and enjoy a different culture from what you are used to. This is your Father's world. He made it for your enjoyment.

Day 63
Overcoming Negative Thoughts

And do not be conformed to this world, but be transformed by the renewing of your mind, that you may prove what is that good and acceptable and perfect will of God. (Romans 12:2).

The enemy will always try to get you to focus on the wrong things. Is the glass half empty or half full? Your perspective will always determine the quality of your life. If you focus on the negative, your life will assume those characteristics. There is a simple principle at work in the world where what you focus on, you multiply. It means how you see and what you see are very important.

God says, whatsoever things are lovely, true, pure, honest, of a good report, those are the things we think about (see Philippians 4:8). Weigh every thought in that balance. Is it good, lovely, pure, honest, or of a good report? If you acknowledge a thought that is not, cast it at the feet of Jesus. Take every thought captive to the obedience of Christ Jesus.

There is great power in thinking positively. A positive mind-set is a Godly mind-set. Negative thinking glorifies the enemy and diminishes who God is. You don't want to do that. It takes great effort to cultivate positive thoughts, but it is well worth the effort.

Day 64
When Life Knocks You Down

Not that I have already attained, or am already perfected; but I press on, that I may lay hold of that for which Christ Jesus has also laid hold of me. Brethren, I do not count myself to have apprehended; but one thing I do, forgetting those things which are behind and reaching forward to those things which are ahead, I press toward the goal for the prize of the upward call of God in Christ Jesus. (Philippians 3:12-14).

As you read this, every word you pass has moved into the past. That is how fast time moves. Every moment you get quickly becomes seconds, minutes, and hours in the past. You are always moving, even when you are standing still. Life will not wait for you.

You are minutes older now since you started reading this. So, when life knocks you down, do not stay down. If you do, you are wasting precious time. Get up, stand on your own two feet, brush yourself off, lift your head high, push your chest out and keep going. Keep moving with time, and you will achieve your divine destiny.

Day 65
Don't Pity Your Dream

Trust in the Lord with all your heart, and lean not on your own understanding; In all your ways acknowledge Him, and He shall direct your paths. (Proverbs 3:5-6).

Dreams are given by God, so don't keep a pity party for your dream. It will be realized if you keep on striving. There is greatness in you. You were born to achieve, and nothing is impossible for you, if you just believe. Your dream is going to impact and change the world.

There is no obstacle that can stop you from seeing your dream come to pass. Opposition and challenges are steps toward your dream. What God has called you to do will always be bigger and higher than you. How do you think you will get there? Don't waste time feeling sorry for yourself. Get up and keep moving.

Day 66
Massive Success is the Best Form of Revenge

The Lord was with Joseph, and he was a successful man; and he was in the house of his master the Egyptian. And his master saw that the Lord was with him and that the Lord made all he did to prosper in his hand. (Genesis 39:2-3).

Don't focus on those who hurt you and put limitations on you. You are better than that. Don't allow the criticism of others to render you passive. Keep moving. Don't stop because you failed to meet expectations. Keep aiming higher.

Don't just stick to what you know to do. Challenge yourself to greater. If you keep pressing, you will achieve success, and that is the best form of revenge against those who oppose you. So don't be consumed by people who try to bring you down; just keep moving up. Keep pressing forward. Keep going higher.

Day 67
I Am Who He Says I Am

But you shall be named the priests of the Lord, they shall call you the servants of our God. You shall eat the riches of the Gentiles, and in their glory you shall boast. Instead of your shame you shall have double honor, and instead of confusion they shall rejoice in their portion. Therefore in their land they shall possess double; everlasting joy shall be theirs. (Isaiah 61:6-7).

Your identity is not defined by your peers, circumstances, failures, or inadequacies. It is defined by the One who fashioned you with His own hands and mind. You were created by God. You are fearfully and wonderfully made.

It really doesn't matter what the world or those around you say about you. It matters what God says. Believe God. You are a rare gem in His sight, a precious possession, a unique individual who is the apple of His eyes. You are always on His heart and mind. You were made in His image and likeness. You are exactly who God says you are.

Day 68
Giving Empowers You

Give, and it will be given to you: good measure, pressed down, shaken together, and running over will be put into your bosom. For with the same measure that you use, it will be measured back to you. (Luke 6:38).

There is a spiritual principle a lot of people miss by trusting their own carnal mind. You don't keep blessings by holding on to it but by letting it go. Be a river for God's blessing. Release what He gives to you, and in so doing you will make room for more.

Never cease to give. There is a scripture that actually says to give to every man who asks (see Luke 6:30). Give expecting nothing in return. The more you give, is the more you will have to give. God will always provide seed for the sower, so you will consistently experience both seed time and harvest.

Day 69
Going Nowhere Fast

So the Lord's anger was aroused against Israel, and He made them wander in the wilderness forty years, until all the generation that had done evil in the sight of the Lord was gone. (Numbers 32:13).

Life is a series of lessons, and sometimes we are caught in a cycle unable to move on because we fail to learn something needed to move into our new season. We can find ourselves wandering around the wilderness of confusion, doubt, and lack because of our attitude and choices.

Sometimes a journey that should take days may take years because of our choices, but God wants to supernaturally transfer us from confusion to clarity. You must develop the right attitude and maintain a heart of thanksgiving, regardless of what you are going through today.

Day 70
Dare to Stand For What is Right

I will instruct you and teach you in the way you should go; I will guide you with My eye. (Psalm 32:8).

It is not always easy to stand for what is right, but you were called and empowered to. The Apostles knew the consequences of speaking the truth at a time when the government and the "church" was very hostile to the gospel of the Kingdom of God, but they willingly paid the price in standing for what is right.

Rejoice when you are persecuted for doing good and taking a stand against what is wrong. In all circumstances, learn to give thanks because these present troubles cannot compare to the glory that will be revealed in you. Stand for what is right.

Day 71
Failure is Not Final

And He said to me, "My grace is sufficient for you, for My strength is made perfect in weakness." Therefore most gladly I will rather boast in my infirmities, that the power of Christ may rest upon me. (2 Corinthians 12:9).

Never allow your failures to define you. It is not the end, but only a bump in the road. Everyone who knows success knows that when you fail, you must keep getting up. Those who truly fail are those who stay down and accept defeat.

There is no failure that is final. Even in the classroom, you get to re-sit any exam you fail. It is the same in real life. Every challenge makes you stronger. Every failure pushes you harder and further. On the road to success, you will have failures. It is through failing that you learn to live at your maximum potential. It will bring out the best in you.

Day 72
Go Forward

And the Lord said to Moses, "Why do you cry to Me? Tell the children of Israel to go forward. But lift up your rod, and stretch out your hand over the sea and divide it. And the children of Israel shall go on dry ground through the midst of the sea." (exodus 14:15-16).

There is something very interesting about the situation the children of Israel found themselves in when standing on the bank of the Red Sea. Pharaoh had released them after the death of his firstborn. He could have stayed on his throne to grieve, but at that moment, it would appear that God quickened his heart to go after the people. The result of this was an elimination of the option for the children of Israel to turn back when there was a sea before them and mountains on both sides.

Pharaoh's army represented death if they went back, and the sea represented a miracle to go forward. You may look ahead in your own circumstance and not see a way out but if God says to move forward, continue, knowing that He will make a way even where there is no way. If there is a sea standing in your way, look up because He is about to part it. That's just the way He is.

Day 73
Don't Lose Your Fire

Be kindly affectionate to one another with brotherly love, in honor giving preference to one another; not lagging in diligence, fervent in spirit, serving the Lord; (Romans 12:10-11).

There was a point in the Prophet Jeremiah's life when he wanted to stay silent. Sometimes speaking on the Lord's behalf has some very terrible consequences that may be seemingly unbearable to the flesh. Jeremiah knew this well and weighed the cost of speaking as opposed to remaining silent. Many of the apostles experienced this as well. What is interesting is Jeremiah's response after attempting to be silent. Jeremiah 20:9 says, "But if I say, "I will not mention his word or speak anymore in his name," his word is in my heart like a fire, a fire shut up in my bones. I am weary of holding it in; indeed, I cannot." (NIV). Jeremiah could not contain what God had put inside him.

There is a fire burning inside every believer. This is the zeal that propels us to do great things for God, and act on His behalf on this earth. Don't lose that fire.

Day 74
Don't Be Afraid of Success

He stores up sound wisdom for the upright; He is a shield to those who walk uprightly. (Proverbs 2:7).

The Lord says, I wish above all that you prosper and be in good health, even as your soul prospers (see 3 John 2). There are many interpretations applied to this scripture. Some believe that only a selected few will prosper in this life. Others take it literally to mean everyone. I believe it is the intention of God for this verse to apply to whosoever will. If you believe it, it belongs to you. God has spoken this to you.

Within the fabric of your being, God has embedded a desire and ability to succeed. This may look really impossible when you consider some people's socio-economic existence; when the poor are forced to walk the streets, desperately grasping at any hope of life. What has little to no value to us is of great value to them. If you tell them they were born to succeed, they may not be able to see that from their perspective. If you judge your life and future solely by the circumstances you find yourself in, you may not see the bigger picture. When God looks at you, He sees success. Learn to see you through His eyes.

Day 75
Live a Life of Service

Commit your works to the Lord, and your thoughts will be established. (Proverbs 16:3).

Interestingly, when God assumed human form, He made it abundantly clear that He came to serve and not be served. How remarkable is that? The One who created all things with the breath of His mouth by simply speaking and elements obeyed and all that there is came to be; the One who fashioned man with His own hands, ordained and set us forth to accomplish His will; the One whose countenance is so profound that one look could kill a man, would subject Himself to serve His own creation. If this is the example set forth by God Himself, how much more should we be counted as servants in the grand scheme of human existence?

It is in service that we learn to yield, to submit, and lead. The God of the universe took the lowest place a man could take and washed the feet of His disciples. The call on your life is not to be exalted or to assume places of great honor but to serve your fellow man, as God himself assumed that role in the history of man.

Day 76
Keep Your Outward Great

Only let your conduct be worthy of the gospel of Christ, so that whether I come and see you or am absent, I may hear of your affairs, that you stand fast in one spirit, with one mind striving together for the faith of the gospel. (Philippians 1:27).

Our outward appearance will often reflect our inner reality, so dress smart, relate to others well, and live with gratitude and excitement. So will your light shine, and even people of prominence will be drawn to your shining.

Someone once said that we are the Bible that most people will read, so they pay attention to our conduct, speech, and how we react under different circumstances. This is where we get the opportunity to imitate Christ in all we do so people see Him and not just us. Make an effort to look good. Speak well of others. Demonstrate confidence in the day-to-day decisions you make, and shine as brightly as the light you are.

Day 77
Inward Change

Therefore we do not lose heart. Even though our outward man is perishing, yet the inward man is being renewed day by day. (2 Corinthians 4:16).

In studying the martyrs of previous centuries, there was something common among them. They rejoiced in their suffering and imminent death. Nothing could shake or skew their hope. They knew they represented another world far superior to this one, and there is a great reward awaiting those who are faithful. They never lost heart.

The posture of our heart is very important, but it must be rooted in who God is, knowing we belong to Him. We must examine our hearts daily. Seek to develop a great relationship with ourselves. In knowing who we truly are, we begin to know God because His image resides in us. Yes, we age. We grow weary and tired. As we get older, we cannot move as we used to. Our mental faculties begin to fade. But our hearts can maintain its vibrancy throughout our entire lives. It is where our true strength lies. Hope empowers us in a world where external realities are not always favourable.

Day 78
Think Outside the Box

Now to Him who is able to do exceedingly abundantly above all that we ask or think, according to the power that works in us. (Ephesians 3:20).

With the limitless One living inside you, limits are just a perception of the mind. You don't have to do everything the same way everyone else does it. You don't have to subject yourself to the laws of the systems of this world just to get by. You don't have to be what everyone else thinks you should be. Go beyond that. Think outside the box.

If the One who dwells in you can go beyond what you ask, think, or imagine, then nothing is impossible. You can do it. You can overcome every obstacle, transcend every limitation, go above and beyond the call of duty or the boundaries of expectations. If you are caught in the cycle of doing the same thing every day, try to do a little more; change the routine, modify your approach. Do it differently. Don't just be consistent, be unpredictable.

Day 79
Ignite The Dream

Then the secret was revealed to Daniel in a night vision. So Daniel blessed the God of heaven. (Daniel 2:19).

The dream is yours. It is the child God gave you to raise. You must nurture it, feed it, protect it, and take care of it until it grows into the full manifestation of what it was meant to be. No one can do this for you. Your dream is entirely your responsibility, so ignite that dream. Don't let it die. Keep it alive and flourishing.

Dream-chasers change the world and create an impact that outlives them. There are names we can never forget: Bob Marley, Elvis Presley, Michael Jackson, Usain Bolt; they all chased their dream. They didn't start off successful, but through resilience, they found success, and their names are forever etched in the annals of human history. We will not forget them.

How many people have died and are long forgotten that wasn't related to you? Your dream fulfilled is the impact you will make on this world. It is a timeless phrase etched in the tree of life that you were here, and you made an impact.

Day 80
Be A Catalyst For Change

Most assuredly, I say to you, he who believes in Me, the works that I do he will do also; and greater works than these he will do, because I go to My Father. (John 14:12).

You are a trendsetter. You have the instinct of your Father built into your DNA. As He creates, so can you. You can make a road where there is no path. You can speak life into everything that is dead. You have the breath of God living inside you. You can change the very atmosphere that surrounds you. You can affect culture, tradition, and protocol.

With God in you, there is nothing you can't do. All things are possible for the one who believes. Don't let anyone put bonds of restriction on you. You were meant to be a world changer, a catalyst for change. There is divine greatness inside you just waiting to be released.

Day 81
Big Fish in a Small Pond

But the anointing which you have received from Him abides in you, and you do not need that anyone teach you; but as the same anointing teaches you concerning all things, and is true, and is not a lie, and just as it has taught you, you will abide in Him. (I John 2:27).

We may see ourselves as grasshoppers in a world too big to conquer, but that is a wrong perspective. If God is bigger than the world we know, and He dwells inside us, there is an expansiveness about ourselves that we are yet to comprehend. We are not a small fish in a big pond, but quite the contrary.

Are you living to the best of your potential? Even if you answered yes, there is still more in you. You have so much to offer the world, but the magnitude to which you manifest what you have to offer is dependent on your perception. How you see yourself is important to how you function. Twelve men went to spy out the land, and ten came back with a fearful report. They succumbed to the reality they saw with their physical eyes. Only two men were able to see beyond that reality to something greater that all twelve had access to.

If you think you are too small and have nothing to offer, that will be your reality. Know that you are larger than life and act accordingly. The world around you will thank you.

Day 82
Make it Count

Therefore I take pleasure in infirmities, in reproaches, in needs, in persecutions, in distresses, for Christ's sake. For when I am weak, then I am strong. (2 Corinthians 12:10).

The quality of our lives is measured by the quality of our perception. A positive outlook results in a positive reality. The opposite is also true. It is difficult to process life as it should be without a positive outlook on what it is. This is where faith and hope become relevant because they help us to see beyond what we are presently experiencing.

Don't live your life from a place of fear. Infirmity, persecution, bad mind, or any related distress should not be enough to break a believer. We are placed above circumstances, not below. We must walk through fires and the floods of life, but they will not overtake us. They will not consume us. We can have the same experiences as everybody else around us, but our response to it can be different. Our perception of it must be different. This is how we make our living count.

Day 83
Something to Live For

Do not remember the former things, nor consider the things of old. (Isaiah 43:18).

You will live and not die. Those who believe in Jesus never die. Jesus said that just before raising Lazarus from the dead. Lazarus was dead for four days. What Jesus did was medically, naturally, and scientifically impossible. God wants you to live, not die.

God is our source of life and strength. He is the reason we live, breathe and exist. He is something to live for. We live for Him and for His glory. In Him there is no darkness, no evil, no lack, and no failure. Everything in heaven, earth, and under the earth is subjected to Him, and He lives inside you.` That means you have something to live for. Choose life. Speak life. Live life.

Day 84
One Life at a Time

So Jesus answered and said, "Assuredly, I say to you, there is no one who has left house or brothers or sisters or father or mother or wife or children or lands, for My sake and the gospel's, who shall not receive a hundredfold now in this time—houses and brothers and sisters and mothers and children and lands, with persecutions—and in the age to come, eternal life." (Mark 10:29-30).

You are a world-changer. Be determined to touch a life, one at a time. You can change this world by impacting one life. That is how the world is going to change. The life you touch today is changing the future decades from now.

Jesus called His disciples one after the other. He empowered twelve men who left their families behind to follow Jesus, and twelve became 120, and 120 evangelized the whole world. If you pour into the life of one, it will multiply and produce a great harvest. Don't seek to be an influence for a large crowd; seek to find one who is teachable. If you have the gift of teaching, teach one. If you can sing, minister to one. If you have the gift of prophecy, speak into the life of one. You can change the world by changing one.

Day 85
No Obstacle is too Big For You

For the Lord your God has blessed you in all the work of your hand. He knows your trudging through this great wilderness. These forty years the Lord your God has been with you; you have lacked nothing. (Deuteronomy 2:7).

The book of Revelation speaks highly about the one who overcomes. It speaks highly about you. Challenges are not roadblocks. Obstacles are not warning signs to give up and turn back. They are simply an opportunity for God to show up and show off. You can overcome. You were made to be victorious.

The road through the wilderness may seem long and never-ending, but nothing lasts forever. There are seasons and times for everything. Don't look back. Keep going onward. The prize is always ahead, not behind. When it gets too overwhelming, look up. Keep your eyes focused on the glorious end God has already determined for you. He knows the way that you take, and He has already decided what your future will look like. Jeremiah refers to it as your "expected end."

Day 86
New Doors of Opportunities

So I will restore to you the years that the swarming locust has eaten, the crawling locust, the consuming locust, and the chewing locust, my great army which I sent among you. (Joel 2:25).

Someone once said God never takes anything from you unless He has something better to give you. Be patient. Old and present realities are gateways to new doors of opportunity. Job is a very good example. You will get double for your trouble. Our hindsight is limited by our humanness, but God sees the bigger picture. He knows the destination He has in mind for you, and He knows how to get you there. Trust Him. Trust the process. Rejoice in the interim.

Keep your perspective positive. See favourable outcomes and stop expecting the worse. Trust God regardless of what you are going through. There may be pain, undiagnosed symptoms, anxiety, fear, uncertainty, trauma; life can throw a mirage of mishaps your way, but God is consistently faithful. In every chaos, He will open new doors of opportunities, but you will not see it if your eyes are darkened by your present realities. Look beyond what you are going through, and see God working in it for your good.

Day 87
By Faith or by Sight

Now this is the confidence that we have in Him, that if we ask anything according to His will, He hears us. (1 John 5:14).

The conflict between faith and sight exists because what is seen appears to be more real than what is not seen. This is everyone's struggle. Faith believes that what is not yet already is. Sight says if it is not manifested in the physical reality, it is not real. God created the world before anything manifested physically because it was already real in His mind.

The reality you think is not yet is already real in your mind. Paul cautions us to watch our thoughts. He tells us the categories upon which we should think. If our thoughts determine our reality, then it is important we examine every thought. Faith begins in the thought. Sight can work independently of thought. You must first conceive the reality you want to experience in your mind, then faith will make it real. So Jesus says whatever you ask for, believe and it will be yours. Paul caps that by saying all things are yours. Do you believe?

Day 88
The Road To Victory

Therefore we also, since we are surrounded by so great a cloud of witnesses, let us lay aside every weight, and the sin which so easily ensnares us, and let us run with endurance the race that is set before us. (Hebrews 12:1).

The beauty of salvation/redemption is that everyone can win. It is not about who crosses the finish line first. Victory is the reward for those who endure until the end. You can make a rest stop; get refreshed, even move at your own pace on this race; as long as you keep moving forward, you will get there. The road to victory is paved with many treacherous hurdles, but you can either go through them, under them, or over them. Never allow the difficult barriers in life to stop you from going forward.

The realities of life will bring us to a wall, but faith says "There are no walls." We are faced with Red Seas and a deadly army in pursuit, but God says "Stand still." We think we need to fight our enemy with the same weapons they use, but God says "Not so." The weapons you fight with are not carnal, but mighty… Before you were born on earth, God paid the price for your victory. Before you were conceived in the womb, God labeled you an "overcomer." Run your race with patience and endurance. You cannot lose. You have already won.

Day 89
You Are Not Alone

When you pass through the waters, I will be with you; and through the rivers, they shall not overflow you. When you walk through the fire, you shall not be burned, nor shall the flame scorch you. (Isaiah 43:2).

One of the things we have learned in this age of increased technology is that we are never alone. If you are faced with something and you google it, you will find a myriad of people going through the same thing. Elijah went through a season where he thought he was alone and wanted to die, until God showed up and told him there were thousands more like him. We are also surrounded by a host of heavenly beings at every moment in time. We are truly never alone.

God promised never to leave or forsake us. It means no matter what we face, God is right there with us. We may question why He doesn't make it better or easier or maybe give us more satisfying alternatives, but there is a purpose for all that He allows us to go through. He is walking you through a process toward the full manifestation of who He created you to be. It means we are the fullness of all He created us to be, but not yet the manifestation of it. As you go through your process, rejoice. You are never alone.

Day 90
Passion for Change

You will show me the path of life; in Your presence is fullness of joy; at Your right hand are pleasures forevermore. (Psalm 16:11).

Those who change the world are those who are able to see a different reality from what is being experienced, and not rest until there is a change. It may cost you something, and passion is a prerequisite to change. You must be passionate about initiating the change you believe you are commissioned to manifest. If you can see it, you can experience it.

Use your passion to create a better world for the next generation. Change something. Impact a negative system positivity. Be the initiator of transformation and change in your area of influence. God never called you to be normal. He never called you to fit into the crowd. Your passion is a gateway to a new and wonderful reality, and only you carry the fingerprint for that. Don't ignore your passions because your call, purpose, and divine destiny are usually tied to them.

Day 91
Let Your Light Shine

You are the light of the world. A city that is set on a hill cannot be hidden. (Matthew 5:14).

God has made you a light in the world; a light that cannot be hidden. You are exposed. People see you. They are looking at you because of the brightness of your shining. You are a dissipator of darkness. You don't need to speak to create a change; you simply need to show up. Your presence is a shining divine light.

You glow when you walk into a room. People may pretend not to notice, but you are seen and you are heard. Your perception is valuable. You bring something different to the table with your mere presence. Just show up. There may be chaos erupting around you, but show up. You may not like the environment you are planted in, but show up. You being there makes all the difference in the world, so let your light always shine and never try to dim the intensity.

Day 92
Get Out of Your Comfort Zone

Let us therefore come boldly to the throne of grace, that we may obtain mercy and find grace to help in time of need. (Hebrews 4:16).

Those who dwell in their own comfort zones are those trying to accomplish their own will in their own strength. You are unlimited because the limitless One lives inside you. Don't create a comfort zone for yourself. Such a place only exists for those who create it for themselves. Push beyond where you are comfortable. God will help you. He cannot fit in a predetermined box, and neither can you.

Launch out into the deep. Step off the boat. The sea is tumultuous, and the waves are intimidating, but Jesus is not on the boat. He stands in the midst of the chaos in complete stillness with arms outstretched to you. The invitation is "Come." As long as you keep your eyes on Jesus, you will be okay.

The boat is the comfort zone. It is faith untested and uninitiated. No miracle can come from that. Comfort zones are a false construct to make you think you are safe, but you are not growing, and you are not going anywhere. Growth comes from taking leaps of faith. Go beyond the limitations of your own mind and see if God will not show up.

Day 93
Valued Above Rubies

Who can find a virtuous wife? For her worth is far above rubies. (Proverbs 31:10).

In the process of creating the world, both heaven and earth, God also created many precious stones. There are diamonds, rubies, onyx, sapphire, etc. These are precious stones that are widely acknowledged as extremely rare and precious. There was once a being who had these precious stones embedded into him. He was beautiful to look at, and he knew the value of these stones. On earth, they carry a great price. You are more precious than any of these stones, more precious than rubies.

You were made to shine, to be set apart and unique. There is nothing normal about you. God has placed a value on you that far outweighs the value of any precious stones on earth, making you the most prized possession of God in all creation. You were made in His image and likeness, made to look like God and be in communion with Him. You are the most valuable commodity in creation.

Day 94
You Deserve the Best

And we know that all things work together for good to those who love God, to those who are the called according to His purpose. (Romans 8:28).

God sees you as a son/daughter. He loves you so much that He literally gave His life as a sacrifice for you. What they did to Jesus was much worse than movies can depict and far more severe than what the animal sacrifices endured on the same day Jesus was crucified. There is no better gift than God's own Son, and if God gave His ultimate best for you, then you need to accept and believe that you deserve the best.

Do not undermine the value that God has placed on you. There is no existing stone on earth that is more precious than you. It is God who has determined your true value, so renew your mind to accept who you are. There are many times we refuse a good thing because we see ourselves as underserving, but God wants you to know that you are precious, and there is no good gift that He will withhold from you. If He gave His life for you, what is there that He would not give?

Day 95
Empowered for Greatness

Therefore, if anyone is in Christ, he is a new creation; old things have passed away; behold, all things have become new. (2 Corinthians 5:17).

You were created in the image and likeness of God. He has placed some of His own attributes and character traits in you. He has the ability to speak things into existence, and so you do. You will declare a thing and it will be established. That is the power that resides in you. There is no reason for you to settle for mediocrity when greatness resides in your inner being. You are a partaker of God's divine nature.

You are empowered to do great and mighty things in this earth. What legacy will you leave behind? How will you impact your community, your family, and your friends? You are a beacon of hope for those who know you. Seek to inspire those who are in your sphere of influence. You would be surprised how much your life is impacting someone else. Be a light to them. Don't seek to conform to the ideals of culture and society, but stand out and dare to be different. You have what the world needs living inside you.

Day 96
Wired for Excellence

"For My thoughts are not your thoughts, nor are your ways My ways," says the Lord. "For as the heavens are higher than the earth, so are My ways higher than your ways, and My thoughts than your thoughts." (Isaiah 55:8-9).

What you can see is temporal. What you cannot see is eternal. God has wired you for excellence. Failure is not an option. Failure is a bump in the road that we learn from. It teaches us to be our best and always strive to go higher. Don't be deterred by your limitations. You serve a God who has no boundaries, no limitations, and no weakness. He lives in you, so you will not be defeated.

Those who oppose you, oppose God, so move into that which was ordained for you. Don't be afraid to be different and take risk. Great success comes through taking great risks. You must be willing to put your own reputation on the line for excellence. There is greater in you than what is in the world. You are immovable, unshakable, and irreplaceable. God's DNA flows through your veins, and you will rise to claim what is rightfully yours.

Day 97
Become a Better You

You are of God, little children, and have overcome them, because He who is in you is greater than he who is in the world. (I John 4:4).

God lives in you, and He is greater than anything that exists outside of you. The greater one in you is also you. You are the epitome of potential just waiting to manifest in creation. Every possibility and potential of a new world is deposited in you as a gift, though in seed form. Every seed must be planted, must die and be watered and nurtured into fruition. Every day you are becoming a better version of yourself. If you remain aligned with the heart of God and the divine potential you have to become an expressed image of the Godhead as it was in the beginning.

You have a choice: Become better or become bitter. You always have a choice. That is the power God gave you: free will. Your will is the most powerful force on earth, and when aligned with God's will, you become unstoppable. Nothing is impossible for you. Tap into the greater that is in you and the greater that you are, and become an agent of change in a world that is desperately in need of change.

Day 98
Worth a Copper Coin?

Are not two sparrows sold for a copper coin? And not one of them falls to the ground apart from your Father's will. (Matthew 10:29).

There are things in our lives we give so much attention and resources to, but truly they aren't worth the energy. Paul says whatever things are pure, honest, true, of a good report, if there be any virtue or praise, think on these things. It means anything that falls outside those parameters are not even worth the thought, and we know the thought counts. If a sparrow can carry so much value to the God of the universe, how much more His prized possession, which is you?

You are worth more than the beautiful sparrows and the lilies of the field. God feeds and clothes them effortlessly. They never worry about those trivial matters because they know their daily provision is sure. Can you trust God at that level? Do you know you are valuable to God? Do you believe it? God's will for you is good and far exceeds anything you can imagine for yourself. There is a version of you that the world or you has not met yet, so enjoy the process of becoming, and God will reveal you in due season.

Day 99
The Power of the Word

For the word of God is living and powerful, and sharper than any two-edged sword, piercing even to the division of soul and spirit, and of joints and marrow, and is a discerner of the thoughts and intents of the heart. (Hebrews 4:12).

The Word of God existed from the very beginning. We must be careful not to confuse the written Word of God with the living Word of God. According to Revelation, the Word of God is a person. His name is Yeshua (Jesus). So every reference made in the Old Testament before there was a canonized Bible is in reference to the Son of God, and He is living and active in our reality today. If God stops speaking, the world will cease to exist because the Word and Breathe of God are what hold all the cells and particles in place. So there is great power in the Word because it literally frames reality as we know it.

Take that Word and put it in your mouth, and you can change realities. Speak the Word. Pray the Word. Live the Word. Hold on to the promises of God. He values His Word above His name, and there is no name greater. Apply faith to the Word, and nothing will be impossible for you. Speak the reality you want to see. Remove destruction from your vocabulary. Speak life. Instead of judgment, speak mercy. Instead of gossip, speak love. There is living water flowing out of you, so take a deep breath, and speak the Word of God over your life with authority and faith. God will always honor His Word.

Day 100
The Power of Mistakes

The steps of a good man are ordered by the Lord, and He delights in his way. Though he fall, he shall not be utterly cast down; For the Lord upholds him with His hand. (Psalm 37:23-24).

Mistakes have the power you transform you into something better than you were before, so don't build a tabernacle there. Do not assume your identity based on your mistakes. Your steps are ordered by the Lord. He knows where He is taking you and how to get you there.

As we near the end of this journey, there are several takeaways. Never give up. Keep pressing forward. Trust the process; God is in it working it out for your good. Keep smiling. You may fall a million times, but keep getting up. Each time you rise from a fall, you stand even stronger than you were before. This is what it means to be more than a conqueror. It means what was meant to break and destroy you actually empowered you.

Some of those who walk in great anointing over the history of the church have been through hell. They know pain and trauma, but instead of succumbing to the influences of the negative experiences, they allowed those experiences to empower them for greater impact. Great leaders are usually born from brokenness, so don't be dissuaded by the fact that you make mistakes. You are not condemned. You may fall a victim, but you will rise a warrior. Don't burn from your mistakes but learn from them.

Day 101
Make It Work

Commit your works to the Lord, and your thoughts will be established. (Proverbs 16:3).

Many hope for great lives. We want out marriage to work. We seek to acquire a good job, live in a great community, and have enough money to live comfortably and maybe help others. Nothing good comes without effort and sacrifice. It is our responsibility to make it work.

Charge up your life with positive thoughts. Do affirmations. Make declarations. Use the power of your tongue to create the change you desire. You are never too old to go after your dreams, but with big dreams come big challenges, so mentally, be prepared. This should be your mantra "Never give up." If you hold that promise to yourself, it will work out.

Live a blessed life. Give where you can. Treat yourself with dignity and respect, even if others do not. Know your value and worth, and always be grateful for what you have and what you don't yet have. Pray about everything, and go in the name and authority of the God you serve and bear fruit. You are here in this world to make a difference, not to occupy space. You are an overcomer, not a survivor. Whatever you put your hands to will work if you apply diligence, patience, tenacity, and the mentality to always push forward. God is in all things working it out for your good, so keep working at it. You have the support and backing of heaven.

God bless you as your journey continues…

About the Author

C. Orville McLeish is the author of over thirty published books, one of which was published by TBN. He is the founder and CEO of the Heart of a Christian Playwright and HCP Book Publishing, God's Image Jamaica (YouTube), God's Image Jamaica and Impact One Brand, and God's Image Jamaica Publications. He is a Certified Writer's Digest University Copyeditor, Herbalist, Mindfulness Meditation Teacher, Graphic Designer, Social Media Marketer, Playwright, and Screenwriter, and he holds a Diploma in Urban Theology from the Gordon Conwell Theological Seminary and certificates from the AACTEV8 School of Kingdom Mysteries.

C. Orville McLeish is a student and a spiritual son of Dr. Adonijah O. Ogbonnaya (Dr. O), and he sits under many hours of this Rabbi's teachings yearly. Dr. O teaches on the mysteries of the Kingdom of God, the realities of the spiritual dimensions, and our identity in Christ Jesus. C. Orville has been deeply impacted by Dr. O's teachings and mentorship and experienced the love of God, enlightenment, and spiritual awakening to the real world.

C. Orville is married to one wife, Nordia, and believes he will be the father of two sons one day. He is an avid reader, who also likes to watch movies, eat out, consume his wife's cooking, do online courses, spend time with friends, and travel with his wife. His true passion is writing, graphic designing, and publishing, which he has been doing consistently for over twenty years. He has worked as a freelance ghostwriter, editor, playwright, and screenwriter and offers his services and expertise in writing and self-publishing globally, accumulating a large portfolio of successful book projects and satisfied repeated clients.

C. Orville spends time documenting his own spiritual journey in published books with the hope of helping someone on their own faith journey. His deliverance from addiction and low self-worth came through the knowledge of who he is in Christ. He intersperses a very small portion of what he learns from his mentor with his own personal experiences to create life-changing and mind-renewing books that answer the questions of inquisitive minds, challenge how we think, provoke paradigm shifts, and create new questions yet to be answered. C. Orville is a gifted young man with a heart to truly know God.

Notes

www.ingramcontent.com/pod-product-compliance
Lightning Source LLC
Chambersburg PA
CBHW072354090426
42741CB00012B/3031